The Lord's Prayer

Ronald E. Cottle

Radiant BOOKS

Gospel Publishing House/Springfield, Mo. 65802

02-0566

International Standard Book Number 0-88243-566-3
Printed in the United States of America

Contents

TEXT	TITLE	TOPIC	THEME (Meditation)
1. 6:5-13	"Our Father"	God Is Our Father.	When we truly allow God to be our Father, it brings peace to our relationship with others, with ourselves, and with God.
2. 6:9	"Hallowed Be Thy Name"	We should give God the place in our lives that He deserves.	To hallow God's name *in* my life and *through* my life is the highest and best way I can live.
3. 6:10	"Thy Kingdom Come"	The kingdom of God only comes to fill our emptiness.	"In every heart there is a cross and a throne; if I am upon the throne then Christ hangs upon the cross. But if I am on the cross then He reigns upon the throne of my heart."
4. 6:10	"Thy Will Be Done"	We can *trust* His will because we *know* His wisdom and love.	If I believe that God is infinite wisdom and love, why is it so hard for me to trust His will?
5. 6:11	"Give Us This Day Our Daily Bread"	We are invited to trust God for our everyday necessities of life.	There is nothing too great or small in my life that God is not interested in.
6. 6:12 (Also 13, 14)	"Forgive Us Our Debts, as We Forgive Our Debtors"	God always forgives our sin while we are forgiving those who sin against us.	*Forgiven* and *forgiving* are the inseparable Siamese twins of the Christian life.
7. 6:13	"Lead Us Not Into Temptation, but Deliver Us From Evil"	It is not faithless to recognize one's own limitations, it is realistic faith.	"I cannot of myself defeat the tempter in my life, but You can, O Lord, and I praise You that You will."

THE LORD'S PRAYER Matthew 6:5-13

CHAPTER ONE

God Is Our Father

Matthew 6:5-13

Our Father. Before we begin a detailed study of the petitions of the Lord's Prayer, let us look at the prayer as a whole. It falls naturally into two main parts with three petitions in each: The first half is concerned with God; and the second half is concerned with ourselves. It is significant that the first three petitions are for first, the hallowing of God's name; second, the coming of God's kingdom; and third, the doing of God's will. It is only when God is given His proper place in our lives that we can turn to our own needs and requests.

The great sin in our praying is that we are too often self-centered and self-seeking. We are too busy thinking about our wants that we never consider what God wants! We are so concerned about our needs that we lose sight of His will! We spend so much time talking to God that He never gets a chance to talk to us!

This is the great sin the Lord's Prayer teaches us to avoid! It begins by putting God—not us—at the center of things. For it is only when the center is right that the circumference can be right also!

So, the first three petitions teach us of: the majesty of God ("Hallowed be thy name"); the purpose of

God ("Thy kingdom come"); and the will of God ("Thy will be done").

The second part is the most astonishingly comprehensive prayer ever uttered. Its three petitions are: "Give us this day our daily bread"; "Forgive us our debts, as we forgive our debtors"; and, "Lead us not into temptation, but deliver us from evil."

The first of these petitions is a prayer for our *present need*. The second is a prayer for our *past sin*, and the third is a prayer for our *future well-being*. These three short sentences take life—past, present, future—and lay it before God. Sustenance for the present, forgiveness for the past, and guidance for the future—all are laid before God! But look at them again; they do even more than that!

When we pray for "daily bread" and "sustenance," we think of God the Father, the creator and sustainer of men. When we pray for "guidance for the future," we think of God the Spirit, the guide and deliverer of men. These are three simple petitions that take the whole of life—past, present, and future—and bring it to the whole of God—Father, Son, and Spirit!

But let us come now to the opening words of the Lord's Prayer—"Our Father" (v. 9). There are two basic meanings of the word *father*. The first is simple *paternity*; that is, the father is the male person responsible for the birth of the child. The second meaning of "father" denotes a *relationship of intimacy*, trust, and love reserved for one's own son or daughter. To the Christian, God is "Father" in both senses. He is our Creator and He is also the One we trust, love, and follow. This is something that was entirely new with Jesus Christ—not even the highest conceptions of God in the pre-Christian world approached this idea about God.

Man had three dominant ideas about God when Jesus came into the world: the Stoic, the Epicurean, and the Judaic. Let's look at the three in turn.

The Stoic idea of God was one of "supreme apathy." In fact, the Stoics called God *apathes*, which means the one who is unable to feel anything. Their argument was simple and logical. If a person can experience joy or sorrow, or love or hate, then another person can affect him and thereby exert power over him. But no one can have power over God. Therefore, God is incapable of feeling; He is passionless, emotionless, and indifferent.

The Epicurean idea of God was one of "supreme serenity and calm." They went further than the Stoics and said that God was totally detached and removed from, not only indifferent to, the world of men. The gods may see the world, but they are removed from it.

As Tennyson expressed it in "Choric Song of the Lotos-Eaters":

They lie beside their nectar, and the bolts are hurled
Far below them in the valleys, and the clouds are
    lightly curled
Round their golden houses, girdled with their gleam-
    ing world;
Where they smile in secret, looking over wasted
    lands
Blight and famine, plague and earthquake, roaring
    deeps and fiery sands,
Clanging fights, and flaming towns, and sinking
    ships, and praying hands.

The Judaic idea of God is summarized in Psalm 24:

> Who shall ascend the hill of the Lord? And who shall stand in his holy place? He who has clean hands and a pure heart, who does not lift up his soul to what is false, and does not swear deceitfully. He will receive blessing from the Lord, and vindication from the God of his salvation (vv. 3-5, *RSV*).

To anyone who contemplates the meaning of these words they are terrible words! They slam the door to God shut in man's face! For no human being can fulfill these conditions.

Judaism in Jesus' day became so caught up in these legalistic demands that it lost sight of the love and mercy of God. Laws multiplied until they became too many to remember. The heavens became dark and cold and God was far away. These are the three pictures of God that many held in Jesus' day.

Add to this three modern examples and we shall see how man thinks of God. First, Thomas Hardy, the poet, said: "Of what good is prayer when we have no one to pray to except the dreaming, dark, dumb thing that turns the handle of this idle show called life." Second, Voltaire, the philosopher, said: "Life is a bad joke; bring down the curtain, the farce is done!" Third, H. G. Wells, the novelist, painted the picture of a man defeated by the stress and strain of life. His doctor told him his only hope of retaining his sanity was to find peace in God. "What—that—up there?—I would as soon think of cooling my throat with the Milky Way or of shaking hands with the stars!"

These are the verdicts of men who do not know God as Jesus Christ reveals Him.

The Stoic sees Him as emotionless; the Epicurean sees Him as detached; the Old Testament sees Him as unapproachable; and the modern man sees Him as empty, futile, "up there."

But now let us see God as Jesus Christ knew Him and showed Him to men! Jesus called God, "Abba, Father." As He prayed in Gethsemane our Lord said: "Abba, Father, . . . not my will but thine be done" (see Mark 14:36; Luke 22:42). *Abba* means much more than just "father"! *Abba* was the word a little Jewish child in Palestine used to address his father around the home; in Arabic it is still used (*jabba*). There is only one possible English translation of this word today—"Daddy."

Yes, this is what was new about Jesus. There is absolutely no parallel to this in Jewish literature anywhere. Jesus came to God with the simple love and trust of a child coming to his father whom he knows loves him! And the apostle Paul understood this when he told us that we too can come to God in this same way!

> For ye have not received the spirit of bondage again to fear; but ye have received the Spirit of adoption, whereby we cry, Abba, Father. . . . And because ye are sons, God hath sent forth the Spirit of his Son into your hearts, crying, Abba Father (Romans 8:15; Galatians 4:6).

How different this is from the unfeeling God of Stoicism, the detached God of Epicureanism, the otherworldly God of Judaism, and the empty God of modernism.

God is our Father. When we learn this it inevitably settles the three greatest *relationships of this life*.

First, it settles our *relationship to our fellowmen*. If God is truly "Father," then He is Father of all! The Lord's Prayer does not teach us to pray "my Father"—it teaches us to pray "our Father." "I, my, me, and mine" never occur in this prayer; instead there is "we, us, and our"!

God is not the exclusive possession of any man— not the good or the bad; not the white or the black; not the rich or the poor. The very phrase "our Father" involves the elimination of self. The "fatherhood of God" is the only possible ground of the "brotherhood of man." When men can accept the simple fact that God is truly the Father of us all, then and only then can there be "brotherhood" in the world!

Second, if we believe God is our Father, it settles our *relationship to ourselves!* We don't have to face the failures of our past alone. We don't have to face the frustrations of our present alone. We don't have to face the fears of our future alone. We can talk it over with our Father; we can put our feeble hand in His; and we can follow His leading and know everything will be all right! What an inner peace there is when we realize God is our Father!

Finally, if we believe God is our Father, it settles our *relationship with God*. There is an old Roman story of a great emperor marching through Rome after a victory in war. The streets were lined with cheering people; the soldiers held them back from the streets.

A little boy darted into the street toward the emperor's chariot. A soldier grabbed him and said, "You can't do that, son—that's the emperor!" The little boy smiled and said, "He may be your emperor, but he's my daddy!" Now that is exactly what we are saying when we pray "our Father." The majesty, the glory, and the power are still all there. But they are the majesty, the glory, and the power of our Father who loves us as His children and invites us to come to Him!

CHAPTER TWO

Giving God First Place in Our Lives

Matthew 6:9

Hallowed Be Thy Name. In the first chapter we discussed that magnificent phrase "our Father." However, in the process of introducing that subject, we noted the two general divisions of the prayer with their three petitions each: the first three concerning *God;* and the second three concerning *ourselves.* Now, as we indicated then, we will consider each of these petitions in turn.

This chapter concerns the first petition of the Lord's Prayer—"Hallowed be thy name." Probably this is the most difficult of all the petitions to express clearly. We will concentrate on what the petition actually said as Jesus uttered it, and what it says today.

First, let us look at the word *hallow.* This is a very special word in both Greek and Hebraic usage. It means "to treat a person or an object as holy," and *holy* means "different, unique, separate"! A priest is holy because he is *separate* from other men. A temple is holy because it is *different* from other buildings. An altar is holy because it is *unique* among other furniture. Therefore, this petition means: "Let God's name be treated differently than all other names," and, "Let God's name be given a position that is absolutely unique."

Next, let us look at the word *name*. In Biblical times a "name" stood for much more than it does today—a code sign or a tag for the convenience of the mailman. The "name" stood for the *whole character* of the person as it was known by others. And as Origen said: "The name of God stands for the *nature*, the *character*, and the *personality* of God as He has revealed Himself to man." For example, Psalm 9:10 says: "They that know thy name will put their trust in thee." This does not mean that those who know God is called "Jehovah" will trust Him. It means that those who know *what God is like*—His nature, His character, His personality—will trust Him and commit themselves to Him!

Again, in Psalm 20:7 we read: "Some trust in chariots, and some in horses: but we will remember the *name* of the Lord [Jehovah] our God." This does not mean that in a time of trouble the Psalmist will remember that God's name is Jehovah. It means that during trouble, while others trust in materialism and ritualism, we will remember the nature, character, and personality of God. This will be our source of strength and courage!

When we put these two words (*hallow* and *name*) together in their basic meanings as Jesus and the people of His day understood them, we learn what this petition actually said when He uttered it and what it says today: "Let us give God the unique place in our lives that His nature, character, and personality demand!"

However, the question is: "How can I hallow God's name today?" There are several things to note here. First, this is a "prayer" not a demand. It is asking for something I cannot do myself. It is admitting that in myself I cannot "hallow God's name," and it is asking God to do in me what I cannot do.

Why is it impossible for us to "hallow God's name"? It is because there are certain "monopolies" in our lives: areas we determine to keep for ourselves and refuse to surrender to Him; areas we know perfectly well He would never endorse—that He would never "sign His name to." This is our real problem. For only a life that God could "sign His name to" is a free life, a full life, and a tranquil life.

Instead, our lives are full of "IOUs to God"—the "books don't balance," and we are in "spiritual debt" and "won't pay up." Of course, God could never "sign His name" to a life like that. But one day a cross was raised on this ugly world; Jesus hung there and prayed, "Father, forgive them . . ." (Luke 23:34). Suddenly God did a strange thing. He "signed His name" to my life. It was still full of IOUs; it still didn't balance; and it was still in debt. But He signed His name anyhow and blotted out my debt, never to count it against me again!

As the Bible says: "[He has] forgiven you all [your] trespasses; blotting out the handwriting of ordinances that was against us . . . nailing it to his cross" (Colossians 2:13, 14).

The second thing to note here is that not only is this a meaningful prayer, but it is also a *promise!* "I shall let Thy name be hallowed." I shall give Thee the place in my life that Thou dost deserve!

First, in my *thought* of Thee. How do you think of God? What does He really mean to you? What is your real image of Him? a "faraway creator" who is busy with other things? a "celestial Santa Claus" we approach only when we want something? or an "indulgent grandfather in the sky" whom we approach only when we have done something wrong and want Him to soothe our conscience and pat our head? How do you think of God?

Jesus said the only proper concept of God for the Christian must include the intimate relationship of "Father." I promise to hallow Thee with my *words*. More than half the verbal usages of the name of God in our day are profanity. God's name is constantly flung from the lips of cursing men. How different this is from the very purpose for which God gave us words and language. In his small catechism, Luther summed up the purpose of man in a few choice words: "The whole purpose of man is to glorify God and to worship Him." One of the ways to glorify God is to praise Him with our words. God inhabits the praises of His people (Psalm 22:3). "Let everything that hath breath praise the Lord" (Psalm 150:6). I will hallow Thee with my words.

Finally, I promise to hallow Thee with my *deeds*. Have you ever thought about the word *worship*? It is a combination of two words: *worth*, which means "value," and *ship*, which means "state of." Therefore, true worship is living a life that attributes infinite and supreme value to God.

Every deed, every decision, and every activity should be intended to worship God, to give Him first place in my life. This is what it means to "hallow God's name."

When we utter this first petition of the Lord's Prayer, let us allow its all-inclusive meaning to grip us. First as a *prayer*: "O, Father, give Thy name—

Thy nature, Thy character, and Thy personality—the supreme place it deserves *in my life.*" Then as a *promise:* "O, Father, as this is done in me, it shall also be done through me. In my *thought* of Thee, in my *words*, and in my *deeds* I will let Thy name be hallowed."

CHAPTER THREE

The Kingdom of God Fills Our Emptiness

Matthew 6:10

Thy Kingdom Come. This second petition of the Lord's Prayer is the central petition. It is the central message and proclamation of the very ministry of Jesus. The burden of Jesus' message according to Mark was: "The time is fulfilled, and the kingdom of God is at hand; repent ye, and believe the gospel" (Mark 1:15). Matthew says of Jesus: "From that time Jesus began to preach, and to say, Repent: for the kingdom of heaven is at hand" (Matthew 4:17). And Luke says of Jesus: "I must preach the kingdom of God . . . for therefore am I sent" (Luke 4:43).

To preach the "coming of the kingdom of God" was the very purpose for which Jesus came into the world. The phrase "kingdom of God" or "kingdom of heaven" appears 49 times in Matthew, 16 times in Mark, and 38 times in Luke. Since this is such an important concept to the Bible, the ministry of Jesus, and the Lord's Prayer, we shall ask two simple questions concerning "the kingdom of God."

The first question is: "What is the kingdom of God?" There are two basic facts about "the kingdom of God" that are generally misunderstood. First, "the kingdom of God" is not a kingdom in the sense of a "realm" or "territory." Rather, it is a kingdom in the sense of "the reign of God."

We often speak today of the Kingdom of Great Britain, the Kingdom of Holland, or the Kingdom of Belgium. However, in the New Testament, "the kingdom of God" is not a territory; it is the active "reign" or "governing power" of God!

When Jesus said, "The kingdom of God is at hand," He meant God is ready to begin His reign here and now, and the kingship of God in His world is beginning!

The second basic fact about "the kingdom of God" so often unrecognized today is that it is *primarily an individual thing!* Of course, we are all aware that "the kingdom of God" and "the kingdom of heaven" both mean the same thing. The only reason for the difference is that Matthew, who uses "kingdom of heaven," was a Jew writing to Jews who would not use the sacred name of "God." Therefore, he used "heaven" as a reverent substitute.

But, the fact still remains that there is no real definition of the "Kingdom" in the Bible. It is described in pictures, analogies, and symbols but it is not described anywhere in precise detail, except right here in our text; however, this definition is usually overlooked because it is so subtle.

In Hebrew and Aramaic writing there is a redundance of parallelism. It is common Hebrew practice to say everything important twice, and the second statement always restates, amplifies, or explains the first. This is seen best in almost every one of the psalms, such as Psalm 46:7: "The Lord of hosts is with us; the God of Jacob is our refuge"; Psalm 121:5: "The Lord is thy keeper: the Lord is thy shade upon thy right hand"; and Psalm 23:1, 2: "The Lord is my shepherd. . . . He maketh me to lie down in green pastures: He leadeth me beside the still waters." In the Lord's Prayer we have the same thing. Two petitions appear side by side. The second explains the first and amplifies it: "Thy kingdom come. Thy will be done in earth, as it is in heaven."

"The kingdom of God" is an individual or a group of individuals in whom God's will is done! This is what our Lord meant when He said, "The kingdom of God is within you" (Luke 17:21). He spoke these words to Pharisees and scribes who thought of God's kingdom in terms of material prosperity, political power, and national greatness. Even today many of us long for "God's kingdom" to come in the garb of social reform, world peace, and material blessings. However, Jesus made it clear that none of these things would ever come until individuals accepted the will of God!

Society will be changed only as individuals are changed; the Kingdom must come in the *hearts of men* before it can come in the world as a whole! We have answered our first question, "What is the kingdom of God?" It is the will of God as it is done in the hearts of men!

Now we come to our second question concerning "the kingdom of God": "What are the qualifications for the coming of the Kingdom?" There are three of them. First, recognition of our own *emptiness*. Jesus said: "Blessed are the poor in spirit: for theirs is the kingdom of heaven" (Matthew 5:3). "Poor" here means not only "needy" but "destitute." It describes the humble man who is unable to help himself and, therefore, puts his whole trust in God!

The Kingdom belongs to the man who rests his poverty and emptiness in God's wealth and sufficiency; his ignorance and sin in God's wisdom and mercy; and his temptation and failure in God's love and grace. The first step for the coming of God's kingdom is for me to realize and admit my own emptiness!

The second qualification for the coming of the Kingdom is desperation! Jesus said: "Seek ye first the kingdom of God, and his righteousness . . ." (Matthew 6:33). Someone has translated this: "Make the kingdom of God the object of all your desires."

"From the days of John the Baptist until now the kingdom of heaven has suffered violence, and men of violence take it by force" (Matthew 11:12, *RSV*). The picture here is of a desperate army storming a city. As James Denny said: "The Kingdom of God is not for the careless and the dilettante, but for the *desperate*!"

Helmut Thielicke preached his sermon on this text in the choir of his bombed-out church during World War II. A few days before, the center of the City of Stuttgart had been blown to bits. In his sermon he said: "Before the war we used to say our evening prayer for God's protection just as a matter of form, with no real meaning. Now when we gather (when we can) to pray, we do it realizing that we may never see tomorrow. There is *desperation* and *sincerity* in it now!"

Then he went on to make this statement: "The greatest mysteries of God are always enacted in the depth! Therefore, it is the cry from the depths that always has the greatest promise." The second qualification for the coming of the Kingdom is *desperation*.

The third qualification for the coming of the Kingdom is *submission*. In Matthew 18:3 Jesus said: "Except ye be converted, and become as little children, ye shall not enter into the kingdom of heaven." Mark

10:15 says: "Whosoever shall not receive the kingdom of God as a little child, he shall not enter therein."

A little child does not fight for power, prestige, or position. A little child never doubts his father's love. A little child will trust his father, not asking to know the way or to understand the reasons. A little child is submissive to his parents. This, then, is what Jesus meant when He said that we too should be "as little children."

"The kingdom of God" is the will of God as it is done in the individual heart of each one of us. The qualifications for the coming of the Kingdom are *emptiness*, *desperation*, and *submission*. Only when we meet these qualifications can we truly pray, "Thy kingdom come."

CHAPTER FOUR

Trusting God's Will

Matthew 6:10

Thy Will Be Done. The most important thing in the world for me as an individual is "to do the will of God." The most important words in the world for me as an individual are the words *Thy will be done*. But have you ever stopped to think of the many varied meanings these words can have depending on who says them?

The defeatist says, "Thy will be done," in a tone of hopeless resignation. He says it not because he wants to say it but because he feels beaten down by it and unable to say anything else. "God is too strong"; too big for man to fight! Why beat my head against the wall of the universe? I can't overpower God!

Omar Khayyam, the cynical philosopher, said of God and His treatment of men: "We are . . . but helpless pieces of the game He plays upon this checker-board of nights and days; hither and thither moves, and checks, and slays. And one by one back in the closet lays."

The defeatist says: "Okay, You win, God! Have it Your way! But I'll hate You for it even in eternity!" This is one meaning of the words *Thy will be done*.

The resentful one says, "Thy will be done," in a tone of bitter resentment. Swinburne, the British poet of the last century, wrote of "men being trampled beneath the iron feet of God—the supreme evil!" Beethoven had a hard life; with a heart and soul filled with brilliant music, he became stone deaf at the age of 49. He died all alone, and it is said that when they found his body his lips were drawn back in a snarl and his fists were clenched as if he were shaking them in the very face of God. It is possible to say "Thy will be done" and yet bitterly resent the God whose will it is!

Reinhold Niebuhr used to love to tell a story about his small daughter. One day he wanted to take her for a walk, but she did not want to go. He told her how beautiful a day it was and how good a nice walk would make her feel. Finally, she came. Afterwards, as they returned to the house, he asked, "Now, aren't you glad you came?" "No!" she replied; "I just came because you were bigger."

Julian was the Roman emperor who tried to wipe out Christianity and restore his domain to paganism. However, in the end he was fatally wounded in a battle and about to die. Historians say that as the blood poured from his body onto the ground, he took a handful of it and threw it into the air and said, "You have conquered, O man of Galilee!" This is another meaning of the words *Thy will be done.*

The Christian says, "Thy will be done," in a tone of love and trust. The child of God can say "Thy will be done" and say it gladly and willingly no matter what that will might be! He can say it because it is the will of God, and there are two things about God that he knows he can depend on.

First, he can always depend on the *wisdom of God.* When something goes wrong with a United States missile, the nation's greatest experts are called to take care of it; the people who know that missile best! When something goes wrong with a computer, an expert is called to repair it; someone who knows all about computers. It should also be this way with our lives. When things go wrong and we don't know where to turn next, we should call on God. *He is the expert on life*. We can always depend on the wisdom of God!

I shall never forget standing at the funeral home with a widow of just a few hours. The mortician said to the mother of three, still in her forties, "I am sorry about your husband. I will do all I can to help you in your grief." Then with deep emotion she looked squarely into the nominal Christian man's eyes and said something I have remembered many times since then to be true: "Mr. Stoudenmire, God never makes a mistake. He always does everything well! It is going to be all right." We can always trust the *wisdom of God.* But there is something else; we can also trust the *love of God!*

He says to us through the impassioned lips of Jeremiah: "I have loved thee with an everlasting love and I shall never let thee go" (see Jeremiah 31:3). Whittier said: "I know not where His islands lift their fronded palms in air. I only know I cannot drift beyond His love and care."

As Paul expressed it: "He that spared not his own son, but delivered him up for us all, how shall he not with him also freely give us all things?" (Romans 8:32).

William Barclay tells of the awful death of his mother. She died of cancer of the spine in such a way and in such pain that it was a relief to see her release. She was a wonderful saint and her suffering was painful to them all. But Barclay says: "I can remember my father coming to me later and saying,

'Son, you will have a new note in your preaching from now on!' " And it was true. He was never the same again, because he learned to trust the love of God! We can always trust the *love of God!*

Our Lord Jesus himself exemplified this third petition of His prayer when He knelt in Gethsemane. Looking at the awful cup of separation from the Father, He prayed: "If it be possible, let this cup pass from me: nevertheless, not as I will, but as thou wilt" (Matthew 26:39). He put His whole trust in the wisdom and love of God, and He left the consequences in the strong hands of God. This is the "master prayer of the Christian."

How about you? With what subtle tone of voice do you say, "Thy will be done"? Is it with *hopeless resignation?*—"I don't like it but there's nothing I can do about it!" Is it with *bitter resentment?*—"Let it come, but I still hate You, God!" Or, is it with *love and trust?*—gladly and willingly walking with God because you know you can trust His *wisdom and His love!*

CHAPTER FIVE

Trusting God for Our Needs

Matthew 6:11

Give Us This Day Our Daily Bread. With this fourth petition we come to the central division of the Lord's Prayer. In the first three petitions we began by giving God His proper place of supremacy.

In petition one we prayed for the *hallowing of God's name.* In petition two we prayed for the *coming of God's kingdom.* In petition three we prayed for the *doing of God's will.* It is only when these have been prayed with understanding and submission that we are ready to turn to the last half of the Lord's Prayer; the part that is concerned with our own needs and requests.

The first petition in this second half seems, on the surface, to be the simplest and most direct of the entire prayer. However, the fact is there are many different interpretations attached to it. Let us review several of these at the outset.

The "daily bread" of the Lord's Prayer is "the bread of the Eucharist." From the earliest days of Christianity, the Lord's Prayer has been closely connected with the Lord's table. In the first liturgical order we know about, it is stipulated that the Lord's Prayer should be prayed at the Lord's table. Some, therefore, have insisted that both Holy Communion and the Lord's Prayer should be daily occurrences for all Christians. One such person was none other than the great St. Augustine himself in the fifth century.

Others identify the "daily bread" of this prayer as "the spiritual food of God's Word." We sing the hymn: "Break thou the bread of life, Dear Lord to me, As thou didst break the loaves beside the sea; Beyond the sacred page I seek thee, Lord, My spirit pants for thee, O living Word." The idea here is precisely that the Bread of Life is the Word of God. The truth is a blessed one: Man's spiritual life is starved and stunted unless it is daily nourished by God's Word. Our minds and hearts are enriched and fed by the study of God's Word!

A large majority of the older scholars identified "daily bread" as "Jesus Christ himself." Jesus said: "I am the *bread of life;* he who comes to me shall not hunger, and he who believes in me shall never thirst" (John 6:35, *RSV*). If we bring these two Scripture passages together, we have the wonderful truth that "our daily bread is nothing less than Christ, the Bread of Life!" Jesus himself is "our daily bread."

We need not deny the truth of any of these beautiful interpretations of the Lord's Prayer. Certainly, the Lord's Prayer, the Word, and our Lord all provide the "daily bread" of our spiritual lives. But I believe this prayer is simpler than any of these. I believe it is precisely what it says: "daily bread" is "bread enough to eat for the coming day." This is a simple prayer that God will give us the ordinary things we need to live in our world. And, as such, it is one of the most precious privileges in life—to be able to bring the simple ordinary things of our lives to God.

God is not only the Creator of the universe, He is also the One who cares that His humble child has enough bread to eat. There are several things to learn from this truth. Let's look more closely at the prayer itself.

"Give us this day our daily bread." It does not say give "me my" but give "us our" daily bread. As in the phrase "our Father," and, indeed, all the way through this wonderful prayer, the *plural* is always used—never the singular! This automatically rules out any selfishness or self-centeredness in our requests.

The greatest tragedy of our present society is "our mutual disregard for each other." It is characteristic of our age that one race does not care what happens to another race; one nation does not care what happens to another nation; one community does not care about another community; and one person does not care about another person!

Life is pervaded with self-centeredness! But the man who prays this prayer is committed by his very praying to care about others! He cannot have "too much" while there are others with "too little." A "war on poverty" is not merely "political" to him—it is "personal." "Give *us our* daily bread."

"Give us *this day* our *daily* bread." The man of faith need not look fearfully into the distant future. He is content to take the present and leave the future in the hands of God. He knows how to take life "a day at a time."

Marcus Aurelius once said: "All that any man possesses is the present in which he lives. The past is gone and cannot be recalled; the future is beyond knowing." John Newman put it like this: "I do not ask to see the distant scene—one step is enough for me." Jesus said: "Take no thought for the morrow. . . . For your heavenly Father knoweth that ye have need of all these things" (Matthew 6:34, 32). And Moses said: "As thy days, so shall thy strength be" (Deuteronomy 33:25). All of these are in perfect accord with our prayer for today. Everything we have is "God's provision of love" for us. "Give us . . . *daily* bread."

"Give us . . . *bread*." Here we learn that the truly Christian man does not pray for luxuries. Rather, he prays for necessities; enough for life. Whenever our desires leap too far afield and covetousness creeps in, we are in trouble. "Things" become more important to us than God. "Keeping ahead of our neighbors" becomes the driving, maddening force of our lives. We then find ourselves caught up in the impossible web of materialism. This is what I understand by the "rat race of our generation."

Please do not misunderstand me here. I believe God wants His children to "prosper and be in health, even as [the] soul prospereth" (3 John 2). However, I am convinced that He expects us to develop a thoroughly Christian stewardship. If there is any single text that emphasizes this, it is Matthew 6:33: "Seek ye first the kingdom of God, and his righteousness; and all these things shall be added unto you."

"*Give* us. . . ." This is the most important word in the petition. It teaches us two wonderful truths. First, God is the source of our daily bread. As Maltbie

Babcock reminds us: "Back of the loaf is the snowy flour, and back of the flour the mill, and back of the mill is the wheat and the shower, and the sun and the Father's will." God is the source of all the blessings of life. We cannot make it alone. "Every good . . . and every perfect gift . . . cometh down from the Father of lights" (James 1:17).

This is the second truth about God implied in this word *give*. When God gives, He gives in conjunction with man's effort! Prayer and work go hand in hand. When we pray we must go to work to make our prayers come true. It is true that the living seed comes from God, but it is man's task to grow and cultivate that seed!

A farmer took his pastor home for Sunday dinner. After the meal he showed him around the farm. Looking over a beautifully cultivated field of fruit trees and vegetables, the pastor said piously, "Isn't it wonderful what God can do with a bit of ground like this?" The farmer who had worked long and hard on that field said, "Shore is preacher, but you shoulda seen this ground when God had it by himself!"

And, so we have it, "Give us this day our daily bread." It is a prayer for material blessings sufficient for a full, happy life. God is just as interested in answering this petition as He is in answering the petition that "the kingdom of God should come" or that "His will should be done in earth." God wants us to bring our everyday needs for bread and the necessities of life to Him.

This personal petition is made only after the first three but is equal to them—the hallowing of God's name, the coming of God's kingdom, and the doing of God's will. It is a petition for God to supply our everyday needs. It is *unselfish* ("us . . . our"). It is *daily* ("this day . . . daily"); an ongoing trust in God; taking a day at a time. It is for *bread* (necessities not luxuries). And it is asking that God *provide* or *give* (God is the giver of every good and perfect gift—He gives as we work). "God is so good."

CHAPTER SIX

Forgiven and Forgiving

Matthew 6:12 (14, 15)

Forgive Us Our Debts, as We Forgive Our Debt-ors. Jesus gives us six petitions in the Lord's Prayer. Each one is of supreme importance. However, there is one above all the others upon which He himself turns the spotlight by repeating and elaborating on it at the end of the prayer. It is the fifth petition: "Forgive us our debts, as we forgive our debtors."

Let us ask two questions of this petition in this chapter. First, what does the petition *request*, and second, what does the petition *require*?

The petition requests: "Forgive us our debts." There are at least three versions of this petition which are familiar to all of us. In Matthew's Gospel, He says: "Forgive us our *debts*, as we forgive our debtors" (Matthew 6:12). In Luke's Gospel, He says: "Forgive us our *sins*; for we also forgive every one that is indebted to us" (Luke 11:4). And, in the "popular" version, it says: "Forgive us our *trespasses*, as we forgive those who trespass against us."

This difference is readily explained by the fact that this is a prayer for forgiveness of sin committed, and there are not only three but five New Testament words for "sin."

The first word for sin is *paraptoma*, which literally

means "slipping across." "Sin is accidentally slipping across the line between right and wrong." This, of course, is the idea of "trespass."

The second word for sin is *parabasis*, which literally means "stepping across." "Sin is willfully stepping across the line between right and wrong." This is a stronger word than *paraptoma*.

The third word for sin is *anomia*, which literally means "breaking across" or "lawlessness." "Sin is the casting aside of all goodness and plunging headlong into evil." This is the strongest of all the words for sin and is really the root out of which all other sins grow.

The fourth word for sin is *hamartia*, which literally means "missing the target." "Sin is failure to be what I might have been." This is Luke's version of the Lord's Prayer.

The final word for sin in the New Testament is *opheilema*, which literally means "a debt." "Sin is failure to pay that which I owe." This is Matthew's version of the Lord's Prayer.

The next logical question to ask is: "Why, if they deal with the same prayer, are Matthew and Luke different?" There is a simple explanation for this difference. Jesus spoke Aramaic and used the single Aramaic word for sin, *choba*. When Matthew, a Jew writing to Jews, translated this word into Greek, he used the word most familiar to the Jews of Palestine—*debts* (*opheilema*). This word was also very meaningful and serious to Matthew, "The Publican." When Luke, a Greek writing to Greeks, translated it, he naturally used the more general word—*sins* (*hamartia*). This word was also very meaningful and serious to Luke, "The Christian Humanist."

There is then no real difference between them at

all. Both are simply making the meaning relevant to their own readers, and that meaning, simply stated, is: "Forgive us for not *being* what we ought to be and for not *doing* what we ought to do!"

Now we come to the second half, which asks: "What does the petition require?" It says: "Forgive us our debts, *as we forgive our debtors.*" One scholar has said, "This is the most frightening prayer ever uttered." The little word *as* is the key. It really means: "Forgive us *in proportion as* we forgive those who have sinned against us."

Matthew goes on to make it abundantly clear in verses 14 and 15 that if we forgive others, God will forgive us; however, if we refuse to forgive others, God will refuse to forgive us. Therefore, if we pray this prayer and hold hatred, unforgiveness, and quarrelsomeness in our hearts, we are actually asking God not to forgive us! God does not forgive on "a bargain basis." Our forgiveness of others is not a "condition" with which God refuses to offer us forgiveness. Instead, it is a "condition without which" we are not able to accept the forgiveness that God offers.

One morning in the middle of the Lord's Prayer, Robert Louis Stevenson rose from his knees and left the room. He had always had poor health, so his wife followed, thinking he was ill. She asked, "Is there anything wrong?" "Yes," he said, "I am not fit to pray the Lord's Prayer today."

No one is "fit to pray the Lord's Prayer" as long as he holds an unforgiving spirit toward another. An unforgiving spirit may never hurt the "unforgiven" but it is certain to destroy the "unforgiving."

Booker T. Washington understood this when he

said: "I will not permit any man to narrow and degrade my soul by making me hate him."

In an old scene from *Amos and Andy* there was a big man who always slapped Andy across the chest when they met. It made Andy very angry. Finally, Andy had enough of it and told Amos: "Okay, now I am ready for him. I put a stick of dynamite in my vest pocket and the next time he slaps me he is going to get his hand blown off."

Do you get the picture? The dynamite of hatred might succeed in blowing someone else's hand off, but in the process it will also blow your own heart out.

The first requirement then for forgiveness is that all unforgiveness be rooted out of my own heart, for "God forgives only *in proportion as* I forgive those who sin against me." However, more needs to be stated here.

If God forgives me only *in proportion as* I forgive someone else, then I will never be truly forgiven; for I am not able of myself to forgive as I need to be forgiven. This brings us to the second meaning of that little word *as* in this prayer. It not only means "forgive us in proportion as we forgive others," but it also means "forgive us while we forgive others." "Forgiving" and "forgiven" are the "inseparable Siamese twins" of Scripture. They always go together. You never have one without the other.

This brings to mind another unfailing maxim of theology. God always *provides* that which He *requires*! He always *supplies for us* that which He *demands of us*. In this prayer, God's demand is that we forgive those who have sinned against us. However, knowing that this is impossible for us to do, He himself provides that "forgivingness" which He

demands through the free gifts of our own "forgiv-
enness"! For God is always busy "forgiving our sins"
while we are busy "forgiving the sins of others."

Andrew Lang, a great scholar and author, pub-
lished a very kind review of a book by a young writer.
The young man repaid him with a bitter, insulting
attack. Three years later while visiting with Lang,
the poet laureate of England, Robert Bridges,
noticed Lang was avidly reading another book by
that same young man.

"Why, how could you want to read another book
by that ungrateful young man who attacked you so
bitterly?" asked the poet.

To his astonishment, Lang's mind was a blank on
the entire affair! He had completely forgotten the
insults and the attack!

Bridges later remarked: "To forgive is the mark of
a great man, but to forgive completely requires the
cleansing Spirit of Christ."

Jesus prayed on the cross for those who murdered
Him, "Father, forgive them ..." (Luke 23:34). What
about you and me? D. L. Moody called "forgiving"
the "most difficult of the graces!" O Lord, *forgive us
our debts, as we forgive our debtors.*

CHAPTER SEVEN

Defeating the Tempter

Matthew 6:13

Lead Us Not Into Temptation, but Deliver Us From Evil. As we indicated in the first chapter, the second half of the Lord's Prayer consists of three petitions that we pray for ourselves. One is for the *present*—"Give us this day our daily bread." One is primarily for the *past*—"Forgive us our sins." And the third one looks to the *future*—"Lead us not into temptation, but deliver us from evil."

As we consider this third petition, we are immediately faced with a serious question: What do we mean by "temptation"? The Greek word is *peirasmos* and it means basically "trial," from the Greek verb for "to try." But it is a difficult word to translate; it includes at least two ideas. The first is of "proving the inner quality of a person or thing." The second is of "deliberate seduction to sin."

If we mean by "temptation" *seduction to evil*, the prayer seems to be contradictory and unnecessary. "Does God seduce us to sin, which is contradictory to His nature and His will?" If we mean by "temptation" *testing or proving one's inner loyalty*, the prayer seems selfish and unworthy. "Why should we shrink from proving the reality of our love?" What then do we mean by "temptation"?

Probably the real answer includes both these

ideas. It is a prayer that God will not place us into too difficult a situation—by which He intends to strengthen us and build up our faith, but in which there is also a danger of falling. This sounds as though the prayer is "backing up," doesn't it?

We have already prayed such triumphant petitions as: "Let Your name be hallowed"—whatever the cost, let Your name (Your nature, Your character, Your personality) have first place in my life. "Let Your kingdom come"—whatever the cost, let Your rulership control the major motives of my life. And, "Let Your will be done"—whatever the cost, let Your will control even the minor actions of my life!

Now we find ourselves saying: "Don't test us too severely, Lord; we are still weak human beings and we just might fall." I don't think this really *subtracts* anything from this great prayer. Instead, I think it *adds* a very necessary and significant ingredient. It adds the *human ingredient*. It realizes that, after all, we are frail men and if any of these great things is to happen in our lives, it will be God who does it, not ourselves.

To state it in simple terms, this petition is like a student saying to his teacher, or an athlete saying to his coach: "I know what you are doing is for my good, but please go slowly; don't be too harsh with me!"

We could also say this prayer is like a child looking into the eyes of his loving father, who is trying to teach him a difficult lesson, and saying: "I know you love me and this is a good lesson for me to learn, but please go easy with me; don't expect too much!"

This is not an exercise in theology or even logic. It is the instinctive human cry of the human heart. "I want to live up to Your expectations. I want to be what You want me to be! But help me to be *strong*, for I have *weaknesses*, and help me to *believe*, for I have *unbeliefs!*"

There are at least three reasons I believe this is the proper interpretation of this petition. First, it expresses our greatest human need. When we look from the past and the present into the future, as we have in these three petitions, what is it that we most need to pray about? Deliverance from sickness? I suppose we need this. Deliverance from poverty? Maybe. Deliverance from unpopularity? Perhaps. But Jesus did not mention any of these! He taught us that, more than all of these, we need to pray for *deliverance from evil*, from the "possibility of doing wrong"!

It is not cowardly to recognize one's own human limitations; it is realistic. There is an old story of a man who had been an alcoholic for many years. But he "got religion" and apparently conquered his habit. However, when he drove into town, he continued to hitch his horse at the post in front of the saloon. It was not too long before he was back inside and drunk again! If he had recognized his own human limitations, he would have changed hitching posts!

It is not sin to be tempted; it is sin only to *yield!* A man is no stronger than his weakest point; and every man has his "Achilles' heel"! It is the mature Christian who admits his weakness and stays away from temptations in that area.

Another reason I adopt this interpretation is that it helps to explain other perplexing passages for me. For example, look at this puzzling text: Jesus said: "If thy right hand offend thee, cut it off, . . . for it is profitable [better] for thee that one of thy members should perish, and not that thy whole body should be cast into hell" (Matthew 5:30). It is possible Jesus meant this literally, but by "hand" He probably meant the work of the hand as we have it in Ecclesiastes 9:10: "Whatsoever thy hand findeth to do, do it with thy might." Thus: If your daily job brings you into situations that cause you to sin, give up the job rather than go to hell because of it.

"If thine eye offend thee, pluck it out. . . . For it is profitable [better] for thee that one of thy members should perish, and not that thy whole body should be cast into hell" (Matthew 18:9; 5:29). Probably what Jesus meant by "thine eye" is the thing you set your eye on, such as your goals or ambitions. One can be so set on social or material success that it becomes a snare to his very soul! If your goals and ambitions bring you into conflict with the will of God and rob you of your spiritual life, give them up rather than go to hell because of them!

Finally, I accept this interpretation because it leads most naturally into the conclusion of the prayer. "For thine is the kingdom, and the power, and the glory, for ever. Amen."

All scholars are in agreement that this was not a part of the original prayer; rather, it was the antiphonal response of the congregation to the prayer. The priest prayed the prayer (perhaps even the priest and the cantor alternately). Then after the final petition the congregation chanted its response: "For thine is the kingdom, and the power, and the glory, for ever. Amen."

Thine is the kingdom. We have already learned that this means kingship. "For You are the King! You have the authority. I cannot of myself command the tempter to leave me alone, but You can; You have the authority."

Thine is the power. This word is *dunamis*; it means "the ability to perform one's purpose." "You have the power. You have the ability. I cannot of myself defeat the tempter in my life, but You can; You have the ability!"

Finally, *Thine is the glory*. "Glory" means basically praise, honor, and worship in this passage. "I do not have either the authority or the ability to keep myself from evil. But, if You will help me, I will give You my praise and worship forever!"

There we have it—the Lord's Prayer—great, majestic, rising to the very heights of grandeur and kingdom. Yet, remembering that "we be men" and not gods, it ends with some of the most human and tender words in Scripture.

"I want all the things I have prayed for: Thy kingdom, Thy will, to forgive my enemies—everything! But, O Lord, I realize my weaknesses and frailties, and so I pray that You will be patient and 'take it easy on me'!"